The Multigenre Research Project

Bettye Montford Edgington
L. D. Bell High School
Hurst-Euless-Bedford Independent School District
Hurst, Texas

Upper Saddle River, New Jersey
Glenview, Illinois
Needham, Massachusetts

ISBN 0-13-052679-7

2 3 4 5 6 7 8 9 10   04 03 02 01

Contents

The Multigenre Research Project

Research begins in the cradle. Watch an infant "research" a new toy. He or she clutches it, tastes it, hits it, shakes it, and strokes it with the feet. Watch that child through the years enthusiastically explore the mysteries of a beach, take apart a toy just to see how it's put together, and tinker with his or her first car engine. What happens to that natural curiosity when the child is given the opportunity to research in school? Most teachers can relate to the fact that students often resist traditional research projects. Not only is enthusiasm for conventional research difficult to inspire among students of all ages, but also the products of such attempts are sometimes even more of a challenge to assess because they too often resemble a mass of voiceless facts sewn together with the sweat of an inmate in a forced labor camp. Teacher and writer Tom Romano created the multigenre research paper while looking for an answer to the challenges of traditional research, which students often perceive as static and boring. Romano writes that he wanted instead:

> . . . the real thing—when intellect, emotion, and imagination merge; when analysis and synthesis are one; when writers, painters, sculptors, dancers, composers, physicists, ecologists, historians, take that which is outside them and bring it inside, intimately, then give it back with form, imagination, and meaning, stamped indelibly with their own personal voice and vision (Romano 1995, 127).

The multigenre research "paper," with its emphasis on student choice and creativity, preserves the wonder and freedom of that innate, childlike need to explore. Comprising traditional as well as alternative sources and creative outcomes, the multigenre product calls for a lively, authentic approach to voice while simultaneously demanding rigorous standards of documentation and credibility.

Possibilities and forms of the multigenre research paper are endless. It can replace or supplement the traditional research paper. It can spring from both traditional and nontraditional resources—Internet articles, visual media, mentorships, personal experiences—and the research can be transformed into as many products (genres) as the imagination can provide. The genres can consist solely of written products, be primarily performance-based, or represent a combination of the two. Students have an opportunity to re-create their researched information in several forms, ranging from such products as poetry and children's books to works of art, a demonstration, or a computer-generated slide presentation before an audience.

This booklet will furnish teacher and student guidelines for the overall structure of a multigenre research project, giving suggestions as well as examples from which the teacher can choose. Taking into consideration the ages and abilities of the students, the teacher can design a personalized project that is open-ended with lots of student choice or one that provides as much structure as the students need. The teacher will discover that the students are more likely to generate products they are excited about once they have a significant investment in the process—products that we hope will be a delight to create as well as to grade!

What Is a Multigenre Research Project?

Tom Romano describes the multigenre research paper as a "complex, multilayered, multivoiced blend of genres" (Romano 1995, 110). It moves beyond the typical research assignment that culminates solely in a lengthy expository paper with a thesis statement, topic sentences, and supporting paragraphs filled with quotations and paraphrases. Instead, the student produces a collection of creative writings, artwork, and/or demonstrations that reveal in unique ways what he or she has learned from the research. Romano elaborates, "The multigenre paper is composed of many genres and subgenres, each piece self-contained, making a point of its own, yet connected by theme and topic . . . " (Romano 2000, x). A sense of unity pervades the project. It is held together by motif or repetition of literary experience. Student choice—curiosity meeting the imagination—is a large part of the success of the assignment.

What does a multigenre research project look like?

Part of the beauty of this alternative research project is that there is no specific format. The instructor can select almost any topic his or her students are studying and customize a multigenre framework to fit it. Student preferences fill in the rest with original ideas for interpreting their researched information, such as performance, artwork, and written products, which cannot be plagiarized or purchased from an Internet Web site. The voices heard through the genres are authentic student voices that, although they may be tentative at first, will speak out confidently as students master the ability to transform ideas and facts from research into creative renderings. One student's topic of inquiry might be a cultural/historical figure or a literary character. Another student perhaps wants to research a contemporary issue; still another could investigate a craft, such as glass blowing. The project may range in length from two or three weeks to the entire year. The aims of the project are those skills that all teachers want their students to master:

- How to find information
- How to analyze and critically evaluate the information
- How to transform that information into relevant, creative, and original products
- How to give proper attribution for information

Following are three examples of the forms a multigenre research project might take for two high-school students and one middle-school student. Each project includes varied sources as well as multiple outcomes.

Example 1: The multigenre research project about a real-life topic

Shevin, a high-school senior who has never had formal art instruction, has chosen to learn to paint in a particular artist's style for her yearlong senior project, which her teacher assigned in the form of a multigenre research project on a student-selected topic. After looking at the work of several artists, Shevin has narrowed her research to the style of Georgia O'Keeffe. She is free to choose the number and types of genres in which to express her findings, as long as her choices include both written and performance products with some "thread" of unity among them.

Shevin's sources:

- A professional artist/mentor with whom Shevin spent 20 hours
- A video in which artist O'Keeffe discusses her philosophy of art
- Books and periodical articles about O'Keeffe's life and works
- A visit, accompanied by her mentor, to an art exhibit of Georgia O'Keeffe's works

Shevin's multigenre products:

- An oil painting composed and painted by Shevin in O'Keeffe's style, with a notations page telling how the art mirrors O'Keeffe's
- A traditional research paper with five sources (accompanied by five abstracts) on the related topic of the benefits of art therapy
- Three classes about Georgia O'Keeffe's life and works that Shevin taught to third-grade art students
- A compilation in book form of the paintings done in O'Keeffe's style by the third-grade students, along with a journal in which Shevin recorded her thoughts about teaching and included pictures detailing the children's progress
- An original poem about art in which Shevin revealed what she had learned about O'Keeffe's philosophy
- Two letters about the artist's best works addressed to significant persons in O'Keeffe's life, written by Shevin in the persona of O'Keeffe
- A newspaper-type article written by Shevin in which she projected what an art critic might write about O'Keeffe's works if the local art museum opened a large O'Keeffe exhibit
- A letter to a community board of judges stating why Shevin chose O'Keeffe and what she learned about herself from her research
- A presentation to the judges displaying the results of her research

Shevin's further submissions:

- A page of notations after each genre giving specific documentation
- A Works Cited page

Example 2: The multigenre research project about a literary character

Enrique is a sophomore who has been assigned a multigenre research paper about any significant character from the literature his class has read during the year. He has chosen the character Michael Henchard from Thomas Hardy's *The Mayor of Casterbridge*. He must choose at least five genres to convey what he has learned from his sources. He may come up with his own ideas or choose from a list of genres that his teacher has supplied. A talented drama student, Enrique chooses products that use his strengths as a performer. Enrique's teacher has allowed his students three weeks after reading the novel to complete the project.

Enrique's sources:

- The novel *The Mayor of Casterbridge* and Enrique's dialectical journal consisting of at least eight entries with personal commentary, which he kept while reading the novel
- Research on critical material in books, periodicals, and on-line articles about the character, Hardy's style, and the novel, with evidence

of such research in the form of notes, abstracts, or highlighted photocopies of written material

- An interview with the school librarian on Thomas Hardy's style
- A video on the life of Thomas Hardy
- A filmstrip about Hardy and his works from the school library

Enrique's multigenre products:

- A creative video of a simulated newscast from the Weydon Priors fair with the reporter's breaking news that a drunken husband has sold his wife and child at auction
- A poem for two voices (Henchard and his conscience) that takes place the morning after the fair
- A colorful mosaic depicting a symbol that represents Michael Henchard's philosophy of life (those qualities of living that he would decide are the most important), along with a typed interpretation of the mosaic
- Lyrics for a song that Michael Henchard might have written at the end of his life. Each of the three verses applies to a different significant period in Henchard's life. Enrique, who is a talented musician, also chose to write the music and accompany himself on the guitar.
- A list of items Enrique believed would be found in Michael Henchard's desk at home, along with a few sentences identifying each item and explaining its significance as something that Henchard would keep
- A copy of the eulogy that might have been delivered at Henchard's funeral. Enrique chose the character of Farfrae, Henchard's rival throughout much of the novel, to deliver the address. Enrique created a written eulogy as well as a cassette tape of the speech.
- An oral presentation before his English class in which Enrique performed his song and eulogy and displayed a portfolio of his original works
- A reflective piece about the process of research and the value of Enrique's products

Enrique's further submissions:

- A notations page with specific documentation following each genre
- A Works Cited page

Example 3: The multigenre research project about a cultural or historical figure

For her sixth-grade class, Cindy is presented with the opportunity to research an important cultural figure who has been alive during the last seventy-five years. Her teacher has given her a list of suggested people and genres from which to choose, or she may choose her own figure with approval from her teacher. Cindy chooses to investigate Eleanor Roosevelt, mainly because Cindy's grandmother has vivid memories of life during Mrs. Roosevelt's terms as First Lady. For Cindy's multiple genres, she must choose one from each of three categories (arranged by difficulty), with an option to add another written product of her own creation. The sixth graders have two months to complete this multigenre research project.

Cindy's sources:

- A biography of Eleanor Roosevelt
- Newspaper articles about Eleanor Roosevelt
- Books, periodical articles, and on-line articles about Eleanor Roosevelt
- An interview with her grandmother, who remembers and greatly admires Eleanor Roosevelt
- An A&E *Biography* video about the lives of the Roosevelts
- A visit to a local museum, which has a display about the life of Eleanor Roosevelt

Cindy's multigenre products:

- A typed list of ten questions (and responses) from Cindy's interview with her grandmother about Mrs. Roosevelt, focusing on Mrs. Roosevelt's impact on women and history
- A children's book about the ten most important events in Eleanor Roosevelt's life, illustrated with original art, clip art, and photocopied pictures of the Roosevelts' friends and family. Her final pages included facts from her research about Mrs. Roosevelt on which she based the story in her book. She also included a bibliography of the best books she found about Eleanor Roosevelt.
- A page of a diary—written by Cindy in the persona of Eleanor Roosevelt—detailing an especially significant day in the First Lady's life
- A poem entitled "This is a poem for you, Mrs. Roosevelt," patterned after the cluster poems from *Writing the Natural Way* by Gabrielle Rico [This is Cindy's additional written product.]
- An oral presentation before the class as Eleanor Roosevelt in "authentic" costume from the 1940's, in which Cindy presented interesting information from her research and read some of her written products

Cindy's further submissions:

- A notations page of specific documentation following each genre
- A Works Cited page

Choosing a Topic for a Multigenre Research Project

Topic selection is the most crucial part of this type of extended product; the success of the project often hinges on the suitability and flexibility of the topic. Depending on your curriculum and your goals, you may assign a general topic area. Students should be introduced to the idea of the multigenre research process early in the year and given plenty of time to deliberate on a suitable topic, one that will hold their interest and enthusiasm, as well as challenge them in some way.

Encourage the students to choose carefully. Often, this type of project is considerably longer than most other research assignments, so the subject of research will be a constant companion for several weeks. Choosing the right subject will make the difference in whether this is just another assignment or one that is exciting and motivational. Specific suggestions for topic choice are found in other sections of this booklet, but here are a few general guidelines:

- Prewriting is an excellent tool for topic choice. Have the students write early and often on prompts that help them narrow their search. Once they have ideas, have them cluster, cube, and freewrite on those subjects. See *Writing Support Transparencies* and *Writing Support Activity Books* in your *Prentice Hall Writing and Grammar Teaching Resources* for graphic organizers to help students explore ideas.
- Build in a "window" for exploration. When teachers ask students to research someone or something new to their experience, they often discover after completing a portion of their inquiry that the topic is not what they thought or that it does not hold their interest. Giving enough time to explore will allow them the opportunity to change to something more interesting before being locked into a topic.
- Early on, as well as at other stages in the process, include time for small and large group discussions about topic choice. Students glean ideas from each other and can usually help classmates come up with ideas for related topics, ways to refine a topic, or even ideas for genres to go with the topic. Make time for teacher-student conferences as well.
- Modeling by the teacher, as always, can give students a better grasp of what is expected of them. In her September 1999 *English Journal* article, "From Mickey Mouse to Marilyn Manson: A Search Experience," Heidi A. Wilson describes the research and multimedia presentation on Amelia Earhart that she uses as a "hook" when she assigns a research project. She says, "My enthusiasm about research certainly must spill over to my students at this point, making even the most apprehensive participants at least willing to give this research stuff a try" (Wilson 75). Becky Ebner Hoag, a Texas high-school teacher who is cited in Romano's *Blending Genres, Altering Style* (2000), reports that her students never complain about their research project after they see the hefty multigenre research paper she completed on the Scottish hero William Wallace.
- Beginning with the first year of the multigenre assignment, ask students to evaluate the entire project when they have finished. Have them include suggestions for next year's students concerning topic choice. Students often have insightful comments when speaking from experience. The next year, distribute a Voices From the Past handout created from their responses.

Acceptable Research Sources for the Multigenre Project

Most teachers lament the fact that the first and sometimes only source that a student considers when a teacher mentions "research" is the encyclopedia. Students need to become aware of the wealth of information surrounding them, some of which can yield sources for research or ideas for products. Even the most efficient researchers will likely scan through a large number of sources before deciding on the ones they will use. Once students have gathered the required number of relevant sources, teachers can discuss the benefits of spending "quality time" with those sources. In a multigenre research product, students are asked to do more than just quote or paraphrase the information. Cursory reading is not enough; students must "peel back the layers," recognize the authors' inferences, and make connections among the various ideas in order to understand the material thoroughly. You can allow evidence of research in more forms than the traditional note card variety:

- Photocopied articles with the student's highlighting and personal commentary written in the margins
- A dialectical journal in which the student briefly summarizes the article or chapter from a book and furnishes personal commentary on quotations from the author
- An abstract or summary of the main ideas in a chapter, article, or video (You may give students a copy of the "Research Skill: Writing Abstracts" guidelines on pages 9–10 of this booklet, which suggest a format.)
- For nonprint resources, a journal detailing the student's experiences and observations, along with dates and times of the research

Teachers need to spend some time modeling effective research skills so students realize the crucial elements of the research process. Weak products are a natural result of a student's not being familiar enough with his or her sources to easily transform information from them into other genres. Here are the most popular sources for research:

1. Traditional sources such as books and reference volumes are still excellent resources.
2. Magazine and newspaper articles for more current topics can be obtained traditionally or on-line, or from CD programs such as *Current Biography, DISCovering Authors, DISCovering Jobs and Careers, ProQuest Magazine Express, MAS (Magazine Article Summaries), SIRS Researcher (Social Issues Resources Series),* and the *Galenet* series. Enlist the school and local public librarians to help students take advantage of the most current on-line and CD connections.
3. On-line sources are unlimited. In accordance with your school's Internet policy, students can print out articles and pictures. They can utilize multisearch engines such as ***www.askjeeves.com*** and ***www.dogpile.com***, as well as sources recommended by the school librarian. Students must be taught how to evaluate the validity and credibility of on-line articles; information obtained from the Internet should be teacher-approved before being used as a final source. "Oh, What a Tangled Web We've Woven! Helping Students Evaluate

Sources" from *English Journal* (September 1999) is an excellent article to help students with the credibility of Internet information (Gardner, Benham, and Newell, 39–44).

4. Interviews not only provide wonderful information but also improve students' interpersonal skills. Teachers can give instructions on how to ask good questions, which are not too broad yet cannot be answered with a simple word or two. Have students prepare their questions ahead of time for approval. For younger students, model a good interview and/or have students practice interviewing their classmates and writing up their responses in interesting and creative ways.
5. Mentorships offer a most effective resource. Many projects require students to spend up to twenty hours outside of class with a mentor who is an expert in the field in which the student is doing research. Students should take notes or write a journal documenting the information and skills that they learn from their mentors. Students need written permission from their parents/guardians to establish a mentor relationship, and mentors should receive instructions from the teacher explaining their expected role in the project.
6. Videos can provide a wealth of information. The A&E *Biography* series can be obtained at many major video stores, as well as in public libraries. English and social studies departments usually have films and filmstrips that students can check out and use to take notes on cultural and historical figures. Some stores have a free checkout section with films about public education topics; specialized films might also be obtained from a student's mentor.

Other effective sources:

7. Experiments
8. Lessons
9. Professional organizations
10. Governmental agencies
11. Surveys
12. Job "shadowing"
13. Community classes at local colleges
14. Museums
15. Art exhibits
16. Public performances

Research Skill: Writing Abstracts

One of the best ways to analyze material from a research source is to write an abstract of it. This instruction sheet will help put the information from the research into a more manageable form.

What is an abstract?

Also known as a *précis* or a *summary*, an abstract is a shortened version of an original text, usually a magazine or Internet article or a chapter from a book. When writing an abstract, one selects only the main points and, as much as possible, puts them into his or her own words. If some of the original points are essential to record, they should be written in quotation marks, with the proper notation of the page number. Taking time to write a good abstract will help considerably when re-creating the researched information in another genre.

Guidelines for writing an abstract

Although there is no "set" form by which to write an abstract, the following guidelines will help in writing an effective abstract:

- At the beginning of the abstract, include the author's name, the title of the article, a phrase that describes the genre (book, magazine, Internet article), and a clause that contains the main point of the article.

  Example: In a *New York Times Magazine* Internet article entitled "Mrs. Roosevelt Dies at 78 After Illness of Six Weeks," an anonymous writer asserts that Eleanor Roosevelt did more than any President's wife before her to change the "job description" of First Lady into a position of power and influence.

- Next, state the writer's purpose. Is it to persuade, inform, argue, contrast, compare, praise, or is there some other objective?

  Example: The writer's primary purpose is to discuss Mrs. Roosevelt's accomplishments and, in doing so, persuade the reader that she had a significant part in creating a new role for women in the twentieth century.

- Reread the article, and then put it aside. Rewrite the information in your own words, briefly summarizing each major point and supporting it with facts from the article. Properly punctuate any material taken word for word from the source, and note the page number(s).

  Example: The author supports this idea by giving details about the active role she took during the twelve years Mrs. Roosevelt was First Lady (43) and even after her husband's terms in office. Mrs. Roosevelt became a United Nations delegate and a spokesperson for the Democratic Party, supporting all Democratic candidates through John F. Kennedy, whom she endorsed publicly just before her death. She could not tolerate injustice and inequality, and therefore she often was viewed as controversial when she became involved with the State Department's policies, many times because she didn't agree with what the government was doing. Mrs. Roosevelt spoke out against testing nuclear weapons and was best known as a champion of the common working person in America after the Great Depression and World War II. She was voted "the world's most admired woman" numerous times in worldwide polls (44), and the author says that "no First Lady could touch Mrs. Roosevelt for causes espoused, opinions expressed, distances spanned, people spoken to, words printed, precedents shattered, honors conferred, degrees garnered" (46).

- At this point, compose a reflective paragraph about the article. What is your opinion about the information given? What is your reaction to the author's purpose?
- Finally, write the bibliographical information at the bottom of the abstract. This is a vital step; be sure the information is accurate and complete. See your *Prentice Hall Writing and Grammar* book for information on how to create a bibliographical entry in the MLA style.

  Example: "Mrs. Roosevelt Dies at 78 After Illness of Six Weeks." *The New York Times Magazine.* 8 Nov. 1962: Excerpts. <http://www.nytimes.com/specials/magazine4/articles/roosevelt2.html>
- Staple the abstract to the photocopy of the article in case additional important information is needed later in the writing process. Highlight or underline any specific information in the article to make it easier to find for documentation later.

Teaching Genre the "Romano Way"

It is difficult to discuss genre without referring to Tom Romano, the creator of the multigenre paper, who feels that "immersion" is the best way to teach students to experiment with genres. Because educators have been guilty over the years of espousing the notion that expository prose is the only "solid" way to serve up information, students are not comfortable at first with more creative ways to express their ideas. Because they recognize that students do not always know how to go about writing a dialogue, anecdote, or yarn, effective teachers allow students time to explore these alternatives. Romano suggests the following specific activities to help students become more comfortable with genres before breaking out on their own to do research:

- Display examples of books written in a multigenre format, such as *Tears of a Tiger* by Sharon Draper, *Nothing but the Truth* by Avi (both appropriate for middle-school age and above), and *The Collected Works of Billy the Kid* by Michael Ondaatje (most passages appropriate for high-school age) (Romano 2000, 28–29). Discuss which genres evoke more meaning and the reasons for those stronger emotions.
- Show students examples of multigenre papers. In *Blending Genres, Altering Styles,* Tom Romano includes four examples of such products from writers as young as twelve.
- Model the skill of transforming factual research into another form. Distribute an article about a famous person, for example, to the entire class. After students have read the article, they can respond with a freewrite or a dialectical journal entry about it. The teacher should model a sample genre for the students, and then let them work in pairs to select a genre from the genre bank included in this booklet and rewrite the information for themselves. Have students share and discuss the power and effects of the various genres. Romano suggests reading a short biographical sketch on jazz pianist Count Basie from *Webster's American Biographies* (1975) and then reading the powerful poem, "Basic Basie," written by Kamau Brathwaite, encouraging the students to respond in writing to the differences in the two genres (Romano 2000, 20).
- Try working on a different genre each day by reading some great examples from literature, and then having students try that particular form of expression. For example, when the class reads ballads from their literature books, students should write a ballad. Discuss the fact that no one genre is better than another; each merely has its own distinctive role.
- Have students write freely about the following topics suggested by Romano, and then rehearse putting their ideas into various genres:
  - "Indelible moments": Those specific moments in one's life that are etched into the memory because of either their exquisiteness or their painful impressions (Romano 2000, 123)
  - "Central acts": Those actions that we cannot separate from certain personalities in our lives. One might not be able to think of one's mother without seeing her sewing, or think of one's father without remembering him in "his" chair working a crossword puzzle (Romano 2000, 125).

- "Crucial things": Those items (tangible or abstract) that some people always seem to have in their possession, ranging from a pipe to a mean-spirited smile (Romano 2000, 127)
- "Meaningful places": The places that have seared themselves into our memories because of deep ties with the senses or because of their association with significant personalities in our lives (Romano 2000, 129)

Once students have written about these ideas as they relate to their own lives, they can practice transferring one or two of the activities to their research project topic.

Guidelines for Product Selection

Once students have chosen topics and completed their research, they are ready to transform their information into creative, personal forms. Up to this point, the multigenre project may have seemed similar to research projects the students have undertaken in the past; now the project will take on a new and exciting dimension as the students use their imaginations to see the information from different points of view.

The following important points will help you guide students in their selection of products:

1. Distribute copies of the genre bank on pages 15–17, and ask students to check any genre that could apply to their topic. Not every genre will accommodate every topic. Encourage students to narrow their choices to a reasonable number, with the goal of having the entire project represent an assortment of genres. The multigenre project is not just a collection of poetry; its effectiveness lies in its diversity. If a student wants to include two or three poems among the genres, encourage him or her to write each in a different poetic form, such as free verse, a dramatic monologue, or a poem for two voices, for example.

2. Because the genre bank is not meant to be an all-inclusive list, have students check glossaries of literary terms for more ideas for specific genres under major categories of the genre bank. For example, writing can be broken down as follows: poetry (narrative, ballads, haiku), prose (science fiction, mystery, fantasy), newspaper (society, editorial, human interest). Artwork can mean etchings, drawings, pop art, and other media. Under the category "notes," the student could consider how a particular genre might specifically apply to the character from literature he or she is researching. Someone researching Michael Henchard from *The Mayor of Casterbridge* could put interesting critical material into the form of imaginary notes from the confidential files of a psychiatrist who might have analyzed him.

3. You may want to structure the project by determining a minimum number of genres or allow the students to choose any number from the list, depending on their ages. Genres can be grouped into categories, such as written, artistic, oral, and performance products, and the students could choose a certain number from each category.

4. You might want to group the products by difficulty and credit points accordingly. When students ask how long or involved each product should be, just remind them that these products are the result of a considerably weighty assignment, so they need to use good judgment when deciding how much effort to put into each portion. Products should be graded for effort and effectiveness, not length.

5. Allow class time for peer and teacher conferences, revision, and editing—all process skills vital for good products. Giving class time reinforces the idea that the student is responsible for making each product as effective and free from error as possible. As a general rule, students respond to the levels of excellence the teacher holds them to by creating better products.

6. Point out to students that, just as the effectiveness of the lead is crucial to any written piece, so is the opening idea of the multigenre project. Romano suggests two important components for grabbing the attention of the reader: a preface and a riveting first-genre piece. The preface, written in the first person with the informality of a friendly letter, should inform the reader in a warm, "engaging" tone of the basic motif tying the project together and of the importance of the subject matter to the writer. The first piece of the project should introduce a critical element of setting, for example, or a character vital to the whole product (Romano 2000, 33). One specific suggestion for introductory writing is to incorporate a picture or photograph that serves as a vehicle to segue into a genre revealing a "defining moment" in a character's life (Romano 2000, 40).
7. Set rigorous documentation standards and stick to them. Of course, students should have a bibliography written in MLA style, but they should also have a sheet of notations following each genre and containing facts, impressions, and ideas gleaned from research used in that piece. The sheet of notations should also have Works Cited entries.

Genre Bank

This list of popular genres might help you formulate ideas for your written products. Place a check mark in the column next to those ideas that might work for you. Add other genres of your own choosing.

Advertisement	
Alternative ending	
Anecdote	
Argument/debate	
Artwork	
Audition	
Autobiography/biography	
Book jacket	
Book review	
Brochure	
Cartoon	
CD cover	
Chart/diagram	
Children's book	
Class anthology	
Clothing/costume design	
Collage	
Coloring book	
Comic strip	
Computer programs	
Computer slide show	
Computer software	
Cookbook	
Critical review	
Demonstration	
Dialectical notebook	
Dialogue	
Diary	
Dramatic monologue	
Drawing	
Essay	
Eulogy	
Fairy tale	
Film	
How-to paper	
Illustrated timeline	
Instruction book	

Interview	
Job application	
Joke	
Journal	
Letter	
List	
Map	
Memo	
Mission statement	
Monologue	
Movie review	
Mural	
Myth	
Newspaper	
Notes	
Official files	
Painting	
Pamphlet	
Pastiche	
Performance	
Personal commentary	
Picture	
Poem for two voices	
Poetry	
Portfolio	
Poster	
Prose	
Readers Theatre	
Reflective writing	
Résumé	
Review	
Satirical essay	
Scrapbook	
Screenplay	
Sculpture	
Sermon	
Short story	
Simulation	
Song lyrics	
Speech	
Story map	
Stream-of-consciousness writing	

Tall tale	
Teaching experience	
Timeline	
Traditional research paper	
Traditional slide show	
Travelogue	
Video cover	
Web page	

The Multigenre Research Project About a Person

The multigenre project is a rich format for a research assignment about a cultural or historical figure or a literary character. This type of project is the easiest to modify for younger students by providing more structure and/or fewer requirements.

The project can consist of any or all of the following components:

1. *Research:* Students are usually required to read a biography or autobiography in addition to other required sources, one of which must be a nontraditional source. Five seems to be the number of sources commonly required.
2. *Research Evidence Notebook:* Students keep photocopies of their articles, along with dialectical journals, abstracts, note cards, or notations from their reading. Attached to each must be full bibliographical information. Although uniformity is the usual rule, learning different ways to evidence the research is valuable. For example, a teacher who wants five sources might require a certain number of dialectical entries about a biography, two abstracts about two of the articles, and highlighted/notated photocopies for the other two sources. Whatever the format, the teacher should emphasize to the students the importance of reading and rereading their sources in order to know the person or character well enough to write creatively about him or her. You may want to check this notebook weekly to ensure student progress.
3. *Process Journal:* Students should keep reflective writing about their progress in the writing and researching process. This journal should include the student's topic-proposal letter, a plan for the various genre pieces and notations pages that follow, questions for the teacher, and comments about victories and frustrations along the way. Any other writing exercises assigned during the topic- and genre-exploration process should also be here. Some teachers call for daily entries; others require weekly entries. Some teachers have students bring this journal to teacher-student process conferences.
4. *Oral Presentation:* Students share with classmates and/or a board of judges what they have learned from the project. They may appear in costume and/or perform or demonstrate music, artwork, or other skills during this presentation. These presentations are usually from 10 to 15 minutes long.
5. *Written Presentation:* Students should include a preface page and their genre pieces, with a page of notations (including Works Cited information) for each. A full bibliography should be at the end. Encourage students to think about attractive "packaging" for this product.

Topic-choice suggestions for multigenre research about a person

Before giving the assignment, the teacher should decide if there should be restrictions or stipulations on topic choices. Some teachers allow their students to choose as a subject anyone who has had a substantial biography written about him or her. Others want students to research only a person who has been alive during the past century, or a person who is "outside" the current culture. Still other teachers allow their students to choose only those figures who have made a positive contribution to humankind. Sometimes, censoring students' choices brings on quite a few battles because of the subjective nature of the teacher's decision. However, the determination about guidelines must be made before the students visit the library or the bookstore. Otherwise, someone will bring in a biography that you will consider a questionable choice. Laying down the ground rules early will solve most problems. One way to compromise is to require written parental approval of all topic choices. Also, requiring that the students read authorized biographies ensures exposure to a professional treatment of the subject.

1. The following activity can help students choose a topic:
   - Early in the year, before assigning the research project, give students opportunities to freewrite about any cultural or historical figure they wish. When the time comes to choose a topic for research, have students pull out their pieces to see if there are any likely candidates from their writings.

2. Listed below are prompts you can use for topic suggestions:
   - If you had an opportunity to have five persons from the nineteenth (or another) century to dinner, who would they be? Why?
   - If you could choose someone to win the Person of the Twentieth Century Award, who would your three finalists be and why?
   - What period of history would you choose to visit if you had a time machine? Write about some people whom you would expect to meet.
   - List influential women in our world. Choose one to write about.
   - Write about someone whom you admire who has been alive during the past fifty years.
   - You are a young person living in the Renaissance (or any other historical period). What significant person from that time could be your best friend because of the similarities in your thinking? Elaborate.
   - You have the power to assemble all the great scientific geniuses (or any other group) who have ever lived. Make a list of the people who would be there and discuss what might be accomplished at the meeting. Who would probably take charge?
   - You have been invited to dinner at the White House because of your achievements in school. In addition to your family members, you may invite one celebrity to sit with you. Who would that be, and why? What might you two talk about at dinner?
   - Because of your wonderful interviewing skills, your teacher entered your name in a contest—and you won! Your prize is an interview with any person in the world. Whom would you choose? Why? Make a list of five interesting questions you might ask that person.

3. With a few modifications, the exploratory writing prompts listed above could also apply to research projects assigned on literary characters. For example: If you were giving a dinner party and could invite five characters from the works we have read this year, who would they be? Why would you choose each?

4. Take a day to discuss preliminary topic choices in large or small groups. As the students brainstorm, have the following items available for them to peruse for ideas:
   - Several issues of current magazines, especially newsmagazines
   - A few volumes of American and world history and literature
   - Authorized biographies of major figures from each decade, including those chosen as the most significant of the twentieth century.
5. Take a day to visit the biography/autobiography section of the school library (or assign the students a visit to the public library). Have students take notes on names and titles of interest. (Ask the librarian to put the books on hold until the next morning to ensure that there are still books on the shelves for the last-period class to see.)
6. Have students check out Internet Web sites for ideas. Some of the following excellent sites have commercial offerings, but all offer free information and related links:
   - *AandE.com*
   - *www.biography.com* (Check the "Classroom" section)
   - *www.historychannel.com*
   - *www.achievement.org* (Check the "Gallery of Achievers")
7. Once a student has decided on a person to research, he or she should write a proposal letter to the teacher and include the following:
   - Defense of topic choice
   - Preliminary ideas for sources, including at least one nontraditional source
   - Preliminary ideas for multigenre products:
     - Written
     - Artistic
     - Multimedia
     - Performance/demonstration

   After the topic choice has been solidified, students should transfer this information to the form, "Student Proposal for a Multigenre Research Project," on page 26.

The Multigenre Research Project About a Real-Life Topic

This type of multigenre research paper is becoming increasingly popular as an extended product, a cross-curricular project, or even a graduation requirement. As educational standards increasingly call for more relevance between what is taught in the classroom and what students encounter in the "real world," this type of multigenre project is an exciting option for teachers, parents, and especially students. Sometimes, this project spans an entire year and therefore accounts for a significant portion of the student's grade. It includes an assortment of written genres from the research but also emphasizes performance or demonstration products.

Following are some suggested components of this type of project. Teachers may choose any or all options when designing a program to fit their needs.

1. *Research:* Because these research topics are usually quite current, most sources will be periodicals and/or Internet articles. Insist on at least one nonprint source. Most teachers require at least five sources on this type of project.

2. *Research Evidence Notebook:* In this notebook, students keep photocopies of each article; research evidence, such as abstracts and notes; and the documentation required by the teacher. This would be the place for a form verifying the hours spent with the mentor. Teachers should check this notebook regularly to make sure students are keeping up with the guidelines.

3. *Process Journal:* Students should keep their project proposal sheet in this journal, along with any reflective writing about the project and the research. Any writing to practice the various genres, explore topic choices, and formulate preliminary research questions should be kept here. The process journal should be a part of regular student-teacher conferences during the term of the project.

4. *Mentorship Program:* Some teachers require students to obtain a mentor who is an expert in their field of study. The mentor needs to be at least 21 and should not be a member of the immediate family. After students have identified their mentors, teachers should send a letter early in the process to inform the mentor about the project and what is expected of him or her. The mentor, who serves as an extra source beyond the number required, should help the student create the written project and the performance/demonstration idea. Most teachers agree that students need to spend at least fifteen hours outside of school with the mentor.

5. *Artistic and/or Multimedia Products:* This component refers to any media, artistic, and/or musical products that the student can create relating to his or her topic. Any artistic product must be accompanied by a written explanation. Electronic slide shows, with several slides to the page, should be printed out and included in the research notebook. These products should be included in the portfolio and oral presentation.

6. *Portfolio:* The portfolio should include a final copy of all written genres, with the accompanying notations page for each. The student

could also include a preface page explaining why he or she chose this particular topic. Any other pictures, brochures, charts, and the like that the student feels will enhance the understanding of his or her topic could be included.

7. *Oral Presentation:* As a culmination of the entire research process, students can make a 10–15 minute formal presentation, reflecting all that they have learned, before the class or a board of parents, teachers, and/or community judges. They need to include the portfolio, as well as any artistic or multimedia products.

Topic-choice suggestions for multigenre research about a real-life topic

Because this project calls for a considerable time commitment outside of class, students should brainstorm for some topics that represent a particular passion, or a skill or subject that they have always wanted to learn about. This topic should not be something the student already knows how to do. If a student wishes to select a topic in an area about which he or she is already passionate, the product needs to reflect a new aspect or a significant extension of the topic. For example, if a student is already an accomplished pianist, he or she might choose to take lessons to learn how to play the violin. Similarly, a high-school student who enjoys creative writing might teach a series of after-school classes on writing poetry to middle-school students.

Whatever the main topic or real-life product, the student must select a related aspect about which to conduct his or her research and be able to explain in the written proposal the relationship of the research to the project. Following are three specific examples of project topics and related research ideas:

- A student who is learning how to decorate cakes might want to research the effects that certain foods have on a person's mood.
- A student learning about photography could research the comparisons and/or contrasts between traditional photography and new computer-enhanced photography possibilities.
- Someone who wants to learn how to install car stereo equipment might research the effects of loud noise and music on one's hearing.

Sometimes, when offered such freedom in topic choice, students will want to select a topic that is in the extreme sports category or that contains some other element of risk or objectionable component. Students should be allowed to proceed in those areas only with written parental permission (plus a teacher phone call!) and under the strict instruction of a professional.

Listed below are some specific activities to help students choose topics:

1. Have students brainstorm, list, and freewrite about things they have always wanted to learn to do or ideas that intrigue them. Reading the papers aloud often will lead to ideas for other students in the class.
2. Bring in newspapers and several current newsmagazines and allow students to browse through them. Ask someone to list potential topic choices on the board as students find interesting ideas and call them out.

3. Have students fill out the Real-Life Topic Choice A and Real-Life Topic Choice B sheets on pages 24 and 25. Some teachers may prefer to remove the specific choices inside the parentheses from the Topic Choice A list before giving the sheet to students so they are not limited to the suggestions listed. Some feel that the large categories provide sufficient direction for students to choose projects that fit their own personalities.
4. Have students brainstorm for possible career choices that might serve as topics or springboards to related topics.
5. Put students in small peer groups to conference with each other about their choices. Duplicate topics among students generally are not a problem because the nature of the multigenre project is such that the outcomes should be entirely different for each student.
6. As an optional activity, have students take blank copies of their Topic Choice A and Topic Choice B sheets home to their parents. Parents should fill out the choice sheets, selecting ideas that they feel their children would enjoy researching. Have students then compare the sheets they completed with the ones that their parents completed for them. Often, students will discover insights about their own interests and personalities from their parents' answers.
7. Once students have chosen their topics, have them write a proposal letter to the teacher that includes the following:
   - Defense of topic choice
   - Explanation of how this topic is a stretch and a challenge
   - Preliminary ideas for sources, including at least one non-traditional source
   - Preliminary ideas for multigenre products:
     - Written
     - Multimedia
     - Artistic
     - Performance
   - Preliminary list of ideas for related research topics

   After the topic choice has been solidified, the student will transfer this information to the form, "Student Proposal for a Multigenre Research Project," on page 26.
8. If the research project is, indeed, one of considerable length and/or weight, the teacher might want to have a "topic celebration." Each student creates a colorful visual, including the title of the project, on a small poster or piece of construction paper and then presents his or her topic visual, displaying it along with the others in the hall or in the classroom until the project is completed. If several classes each period are participating, their displays could be combined as a fun way to "kick off" this project. Having these topic visuals on display is an effective method to "advertise" to next year's students, who might begin their topic search even earlier.

Real-life Topic Choice A

What have you always wanted to investigate? To learn to do? To create? This multigenre research project will give you an opportunity to choose how you spend a great amount of your time and energy in this class. Consider the following areas of interest, which have sample project titles listed beside them. Check, circle, or add to this list any areas that interest you:

______ Science (brain theories, genetic engineering, physics)

______ Technology (artificial intelligence, programming, software design, virtual reality)

______ Medicine (acupuncture, dyslexia, laser surgeries, muscle rehabilitation)

______ Performing arts (clowning, cultural dance, piano)

______ Visual arts (Feng Shui, interior design, origami, photography)

______ Global subjects (global warming, hunger, languages, rainforests, travel)

______ Communications and media (creative writing, filmmaking, journalism)

______ Environment and natural resources (biological warfare, oil spills, weather patterns)

______ Marketing (advertising, Internet sites, trends)

______ Sports (sports medicine, sports salaries, steroids)

______ Transportation (learning to fly, space stations, space travel)

______ Construction (framing a house, metal art, woodworking)

______ Career choices (auto body repair, law enforcement, meteorology)

______ Government and the law (juvenile justice, penal system, politics)

______ Contemporary social issues (homelessness, poverty, surrogate parenting)

______ Social sciences (anger management, birth order, dreams)

______ Leisure and hobbies (quilting, scuba diving, self-defense)

Real-life Topic Choice B

Write three topics you are considering for your multigenre research project on the lines below:

____

____

____

Answer the following questions about your choices:

1. Which topic will hold your interest for several months? __________

2. Which one do you know the least about? __________

3. Which one do you know the most about? __________

4. Which topic lends itself to complex investigation? To layers of analysis? __________

5. Which topic will your parents most likely want you to choose? __________

6. What will the research for each topic cost? __________

7. Which topic connects most closely with your future career? __________

8. Which topic will stretch/challenge you the most? __________

9. Which topic represents something you've always wanted to do? __________

10. Which topic is the biggest challenge to you? __________

In the space below, write about the topic you're considering. Comment on the possibilities as well as the limitations.

____

Student Proposal for a Multigenre Research Project

Student Name: ____________________

For my project, I have chosen to

____

____

____

My research will be about the following related topic (if applicable):

____

____

Possible genres (written, artistic, multimedia, and/or demonstration) that I will consider:

____

____

____

____

____

____

The person who will serve as my mentor will be (if applicable):

Name ____________________

Position ____________________

Phone number ____________________

E-mail address ____________________

Relationship to me ____________________

I have read and am aware of the requirements for the components of the multigenre research project. I approve of my child's project choice and mentor choice (if applicable) listed above.

Parent's signature ____________________

Parent's phone ____________________

Parent's e-mail____________________

Assessing the Multigenre Project

Effective teachers link their assessment instruments to the goals and objectives of the assignment. Because having the students learn to carry out the process of research effectively is the primary aim of any research project, much of the grade should reflect those skills. Students can help create the assessment instrument by having a voice in determining the components that they think are most important in the assessment. Giving students at the beginning of the research project the rubric with which they will be assessed always helps them see the "big picture" of the assignment and focus on those areas that carry the most weight.

Here is an example of the percentage breakdown of one teacher's evaluation instrument on a research project about a real-life topic:

Research Evidence Notebook: 20%
Process Journal: 10%
Portfolio With Written Genres: 40%
Oral Presentation: 30%

The research and process journals could be graded on completion and thoroughness of documentation; genre pieces could be graded on originality, variety, effort, and relationship to research. Oral presentations should exhibit effort, enthusiasm, accuracy and depth of information, and overall poise and preparedness of the presenter.

Many teachers also include as part of the grade the student's written evaluation at the culmination of the project. When the student has expended a great deal of time and effort on a project, the usual result is a feeling of ownership and investment in it. It is therefore quite appropriate to allow the student to participate in the evaluation. This student-evaluated portion of the grade could come as a part of the Process Journal or could be a separate component.

Bibliography

Avi. *Nothing but the Truth.* New York: Avon, 1991.

Brathwaite, Edward Kamau. *Jah Music.* Mona, Kingston 7, Jamaica: Savacou Cooperative, 1986.

Draper, Sharon. *Tears of a Tiger.* New York: Atheneum, 1994.

Gardner, Susan A., Hiltraut H. Benham, and Bridget M. Newell. "Oh, What a Tangled Web We've Woven! Helping Students Evaluate Sources." *English Journal* Sept. 1999: 39–44.

Grierson, Sirpa T. "Circling Through Text: Teaching Research Through Multigenre Writing." *English Journal* Sept. 1999: 51–55.

Hardy, Thomas. *The Mayor of Casterbridge.* New York: Bantam Books, 1981.

Macrorie, Ken. *The I-Search Paper.* Portsmouth, NH: Boynton/Cook, 1983.

Nicolini, Mary B. "Pictures of an Exhibition: Senior Graduation Exit Projects as Authentic Research." *English Journal* Sept. 1999: 91–98.

Ondaatje, Michael. *The Collected Works of Billy the Kid.* New York: Penguin, 1984. Original edition, Toronto: House of Anansi Press, 1970.

Rico, Gabrielle. *Writing the Natural Way: Using Right-Brain Techniques to Release Your Expressive Powers.* New York: Jeremy P. Tarcher, Putnam, 1983.

Romano, Tom. *Writing with Passion: Life Stories, Multiple Genres.* Portsmouth, NH: Boynton/Cook, 1995.

_________. *Blending Genres, Altering Styles.* Portsmouth, NH: Boynton/Cook, 2000.

"Thomas Hardy." *Famous Authors Series* #1807. West Long Branch, New Jersey: Kultur International Films.

Wilson, Heidi A., with Frank L. Castner. "From Mickey Mouse to Marilyn Manson: A Search Experience." *English Journal* Sept. 1999: 74–81.

Appendix: Multigenre Samples

On the following pages are examples of multigenre products by senior advanced-placement student Brandy Ashcraft from L. D. Bell High School in Hurst, Texas. Brandy is passionate about the poetry of E. E. Cummings, so he was her first choice when she was faced with a decision about a topic for her yearlong senior project. Five of her creative genre pieces are included here:

1. "Difference of Opinion"—a poem for two voices that could have been written by E. E. Cummings and a critic about the role of structure in writing poetry, along with an analysis of the poem's style and meaning
2. A list of items that could have been found in Cummings's briefcase, along with a page telling how each related to his life
3. A letter to a newspaper that could have been written by Mrs. Cummings about Cummings's lower case letters, plus explanations
4. A poem that could have been written by E. E. Cummings about his opinion of writing forms, along with an analysis and research notes
5. Several entries that could have been written by Cummings in his personal diary at a young age, plus a page of notations detailing why the author chose to write creatively about Cummings's youth in this manner

These represent only a portion of Brandy's multigenre research project. She also completed these additional activities for her project:

- A traditional research paper analyzing Cummings's poetic style and its impact on modern poets
- An illustrated anthology of original poetry, professionally bound
- Pictures of a series of six creative writing classes planned and taught weekly at night by Brandy to peers and adults
- A 15-minute oral presentation entitled "E. E. Cummings—He Who Dared to Call Himself a Man" to a board of community judges.

1. Difference of Opinion

E. E. Cummings	Poetry Critic
poetry is life	Poetry is life.
i wrote for myself	
no one else needs	
to understand	To understand
	a poem,
	it is necessary to analyze
	rhyme and meter.
what i feel	
technique and style	Technique and style
is	are
not	
everything	everything
	in
poetry	poetry.
should allude to	
beauty pain intricacy	
exhilaration wonder of life	
	Hmph . . .
aren't all those human juices	
important anymore?	
my style	Your style
is humanity that	
can't be explained	can't be explained.
nothing in life is ever completely	
clear	Clearly
	a sign of underdevelopment.
a pity	A pity.
i liked	
my glasses	
	He had signs of real talent . . .

"So far as I am concerned, poetry and every other art was and is and forever will be strictly and distinctly a question of individuality . . . poetry is being, not doing. If you wish to follow, even at a distance, the poet's calling . . . you've got to come out of the measurable doing universe into the immeasurable house of being . . . Nobody else can be alive for you; nor can you be alive for anybody else."

—E. E. Cummings

Analysis of "Difference of Opinion"

E. E. Cummings was a poet known for his passion and strong belief in living life in the *carpe diem* mode. Although he did not consider his style difficult or complicated, he did believe that most people in the world simply wouldn't get his work precisely because they were "mostpeople." In his introduction to "New Poems," a section from *E. E. Cummings: Complete Poems 1904–1962*, Cummings writes:

"The poems to come are for you and me and are not for mostpeople—it's no use trying to pretend that mostpeople and ourselves are alike. . . . You and I are human beings; mostpeople are snobs. . . . If most people were to be born twice, they'd improbably call it dying—you and I are not snobs. We can never be born enough. . . . Life, for mostpeople, simply isn't."

This two-voice poem simply compares Cummings's view on the beauty of art to the ideas of one of his nameless stronger critics that found fault in his confusing technique that seemed to be nonsense. Both sides seem to be pretty straightforward except maybe the last line by Cummings that reads "a pity/i liked/my glasses." This line is in reference to the critic's comment that he was underdeveloped in his writing since it was unexplainable. Basically, an exasperated Cummings sarcastically remarks that he was seeing the world more clearly through his myriad of wild words than the critic ever would with his strong emphasis on rhyme and reason. While some of his works may look confusing upon first glance, Cummings's work does seem to throw a new light on old subjects, thus acting as sort of a pair of glasses.

2. Things Found in E. E. Cummings's Briefcase

- Krazy Kat comics
- Harvard alumni newsletter
- Greek manuscript
- Scribbled thoughts on a napkin
- Dogtags
- Edited scripts to plays
- Wedding pictures
- Art sketches
- Newspaper article on Russia
- French poetry
- Chinese characters dictionary

Explanation of Things Found in E. E. Cummings's Briefcase

All the items listed in the briefcase do have a relation to the actual life and hobbies of E. E. Cummings:

- This eccentric poet was a big fan of Krazy Kat comics, and even wrote an introduction for a collection of such comics.
- Since he had grown up just down the road from Harvard, it was no surprise that Cummings would make this his alma mater, graduating magna cum laude and delivering a commencement speech entitled, "The New Art."
- He majored in Classical Studies at Harvard, where he spent a great deal of time translating old Greek manuscripts. Historians believe this experience had an influence on his style, since the Greeks used little punctuation or capitalization.
- Cummings was also known to have an erratic mind that jumped around with thoughts so much that he would scribble down thoughts wherever he was.
- During World War I, Cummings worked in France on a medical team until he was arrested for suspected treason. After being released on New Year's Day, 1918, Cummings was drafted into the U.S. army and served until the armistice was declared.
- Besides his poetry, Cummings was also famous for his plays and artwork that appeared in the magazine, *The Dial.*
- Married three times, Cummings apparently only found happiness in his last marriage, to Marion.
- Since he had worked in France, he was also known to translate French poetry into English and vice versa.
- Since Cummings wrote during the rise of Communism, it was no surprise that several of his poems alluded to current Russian issues, such as Stalin's Five-Year Plan and the purges of the time that went unnoticed. Cummings also made a trip to Russia in 1931.
- Lastly, he was known for having a love for Chinese calligraphy and a fascination with Asian culture that led to a Japanese quality to his artwork.

3. Letter to a Newspaper From Marion Cummings

Dear Editors of the poetry of E. E. Cummings:

It has distressed me greatly to see that since the tragic death of my husband, the publishers have persisted in leaving his name spelled in the lower case, e. e. cummings. I have written this letter to dispel this myth and any other rumors that have developed around his name. To begin with, the notion that he had his name legally changed to have no capital letters is not only absurd but also purely laughable.

How this rumor came about and managed to persist all these years still eludes me. It is my impression that this mix-up first began with an editor's misinterpretation of his handwriting that indeed did make his name look bare of capital letters. After a while, it didn't seem to matter any more since it was a notion people had begun to associate with my husband. But since he is now gone and buried, I would greatly appreciate it if you respect this old widow's request and print his name the right way with capital letters from here on out. The gesture means a great deal to me. Thank you.

Sincerely yours,

Marion Cummings

Explanation of the Letter From Marion Cummings

For some absurd reason, the capitalization of E. E. Cummings's name was under serious debate for many decades following his death. Finally, his last wife, Marion, requested that this grievous misuse of capitalization be rectified since it was inaccurate. Despite the fact that many people now recognize his name in the proper fashion, there are still those who persist in leaving his name in the nonconformist spelling of eecummings.

4. E. E. Cummings's Opinion About Writing Forms

I.

rhyming is a form of teaching Jezebel im writing a villanelle
ringggigngignggngngingginininiringiginigingngrrring
not knowing where friends education fell

parents wisha mind they forget to do so well
singgsingsignsgignsingsingsignignsinsignsignsigsing
rhyming is a form of teaching Jezebel im writing a villanelle

wondrous minds touch the thoughts they never expel
thinggingthinghtihinthttttthgthintthitnthtihthtihthingthing
not knowing where friends education fell

some brain knew the thought process would never sell
chachingchahchingchacngchachchchchachachingchaching
rhyming is a form of teaching Jezebel im writing a villanelle

succinct ending makes that tone reverberating bell
escapingepapacpapinpaggpagapngpinginescaping
rhyming is a form of teaching Jezebel im writing a villanelle
not knowing where friends education fell

"The relation of an artist to his audience is neither positive nor negative It's at right angles I'm not writing 'difficult' so that simple people won't understand me I'm not writing 'difficult' for difficult people to understand Insofar as I have any conception of my audience, it inhibits me An audience directs things its own way." —E. E. Cummings

Analysis and Research Notes for E. E. Cummings's Opinion About Writing Forms

This poem is one that could have been written by E. E. Cummings. I think he might have written this poem as a villanelle, a poetry structure of sixteen lines with two different rhymes used in repetition, a more famous example being Dylan Thomas's "Do Not Go Gentle Into That Good Night." The use of repetition in a villanelle can consequently bring about a boring, nostalgic poem. I gathered through my research that although he was known to use rhyme schemes and rhythms, Cummings could have had a sense of false mockery about formulas as defined by literary examples. With this villanelle that was "written" by Cummings, there are two points being made: one, about the way in which Cummings perceives how education is sometimes received by students still in the process of discovering their minds, and the next, about the way a poem can be so easily defined in the style in which it is presented.

Stanza One: The first line of the poem, which is to be repeated quite often, has an allusion to Jezebel, a biblical temptress, implying that by being taught about rhyming, one is tempted to give in to the idea of rhyming. This thought is concluded with a run-on thought that the writer has given in to the temptation and is writing the formulaic villanelle.

Chaotic repetition of the word *ring* symbolizes the confusing beginning of school, which usually starts with a bell. As the poem progresses, this middle chaos is never resolved, revealing the state of pandemonium in which people live their lives, never quite grasping a single thought in its singular form. The next repeated line is a direct statement of the idea that one can never be quite sure where all the facts and years of numbers and words have gone in the minds of students.

Stanza Two: Next, we see the characteristic not-quite-critical remark on parents that is seen often throughout Cummings's works. Here, the parents have apparently lost track of their children's minds, but they still hope their children succeed at school. Repetition of the word *sing* implies that the parents are singing praises to the education of their children. This glory is quickly cut off with the once-again-repeated idea that this education is becoming standardized.

Stanza Three: Cummings was known for his simple appreciation for the glory of what the mind could produce. This idea is portrayed here with the thought that the expanding minds of the students can tap into the experiences of life; they can never be rid of these ideas. The word *thing* is showered throughout the next line to relate to the ideas from the first sentence. Although the next line has been seen before, the new repetition of this line has a more melancholy tone, suggesting that the wonder found in the first line has been lost throughout the drilling education process.

Stanza Four: An ambiguous brain serves as an omnipotent presence that had already predicted that an individual would not fit in with formula teaching. Repeating the word *chaching,* a cash register's sound, serves as a link to the reference to selling education. Once again, the repetition of the first line links the idea that teaching styles is part of that process that sometimes doesn't appeal to students.

Stanza Five: The disjointed sentence that begins the next stanza displays the abrupt ending to the education that has become such a part of a student's life. The adjective *reverberating* introduces the idea that although our education can seem unconnected and quickly over, it will continue to echo throughout life. The word *escape* actually seems to be attempting to escape its own confused self. This word, when placed before the repeated rhyming line, indicates that an escape is being attempted—away from the rigid lessons. Finally, the last sentence, repeated from stanza three, takes on another meaning of hopelessness to find an original idea since escape seemed impossible.

5. Excerpts From E. E. Cummings's Grade-School Diary

October 3, 1904

We had a sub today. She was quite ordinary. I'm sure it isn't fair to assume that from merely one day, but I do. She treated us like regular kids, as if our capacity to knowledge had diminished with her coming. I wonder if we'll all look like that in our frumpy old age: void and empty of reason and independence. Boy, how I hate that kind. I never want to lose my mind, it seems so important. She disapproved of our lively minds and action. I wonder if she realized we were the "smart" class. Well, I suppose I now know how it feels to be everyone else, just like everyone else. Loss of creativity is quite draining.

October 14, 1904

Happy birthday, Zeus.

December 12, 1904

Today I caused a minor riot in the cafeteria. It wasn't like I meant to. . . . It all began as I couldn't get to my seat at my table due to overcrowded aisles. . . . So I walked on the back of chairs balancing my food carefully on my hand. I didn't spill anything but was ordered down by a teacher anyway. I thought, well it really isn't my fault; it shouldn't be so crowded. Overcrowded schools are not my problem. I didn't do anything wrong. Nothing wrong. So people protested, and before I knew it, food was flying for no particular reason but to see what more trouble it could cause. Got good friends, I guess. Man oh man, those mini-riots are fun. But I still got in trouble because society has taught us that chairs are for sitting not walking on the backs of.

January 1, 1905

Happy New Year, little boy blue.

February 21, 1905

Today in history we went over American patriotism. For this we were required to learn several songs of strong patriotism. It made me feel proud to be a member of such a wonderful country that could offer such a free life for so many people. I wonder how someone else would feel had he seen us standing up in our wrinkled pants with our hands on our hearts swaying to an invisible beat started by an overzealous woman who almost seemed to cry at the sound of our frail voices. Would he think us wonderful images of patriotism or monkeys with rhythm?

November 18, 1910

I am a lanky boy of sixteen now, I haven't written in this old thing in a great while. What a fiery child I was! Maybe I still am that small child as I don't remember growing up. The reason I'm really writing is to announce that I met my Lady, the girl I have been longing for. Furthermore, I plan on attending Harvard next year. I have a strange feeling that I will lose track of my Lady as time goes on.

Writer's Notations About Excerpts From E. E. Cummings's Grade-School Diary

It is hard to clearly grasp how such an idiosyncratic writer would have behaved as a child, but I have tried to give the image I have obtained from different perspectives. Here, Cummings is portrayed as a slightly rebellious youth still trying to figure out who he was. The last entry has an allusion to a figure in Cummings's poetry that caused many critics to simply dismiss his love poetry as ambiguous and meaningless. Some of his love poetry is disregarded so easily, mainly because nearly all alludes to someone he calls "Lady." I have no historical background to support who that "Lady" could have been or when he met her, but I feel that it must have been someone he loved quite dearly.

BIBLIOGRAPHY

"An Unofficial E. E. Cummings Starting Point."
<http://members.tripod.com/~DWipf/cummings.html> March 2000.

"e e cummings—Biographical Timeline."
<http://www.geocities.com/SoHo/8454/bio.htm>

e. e. cummings. "e. e. cummings on Krazy Kat." *A Miscellany Revised.* Ed. George J. Firmage. New York: Liveright Publishing Company, 1974.

E. E. Cummings. *E. E. Cummings: Complete Poems 1904–1962.* Ed. George J. Firmage. New York: Liveright Publishing Company, 1997.

"E. E. Cummings and Gertrude Stein."
<http://www.library.yale.edu/beinecke/orient/mod11.htm>
Yale University: Beinecke Rare Book and Manuscript Library, 1997.

Friedman, Norman. "NOT 'e. e. cummings.'" *Spring—The Journal of the E. E. Cummings Society,* volume 1, 1992.
<http://www.gvsu.edu/english/Cummings/Index.htm> pp. 114–121.

K. Kaupunginkirjasto. "e e cummings (1894–1962)—Edward Estlin Cummings." <http://www.kirjasto.sci.fi/cummings.htm> 1997.